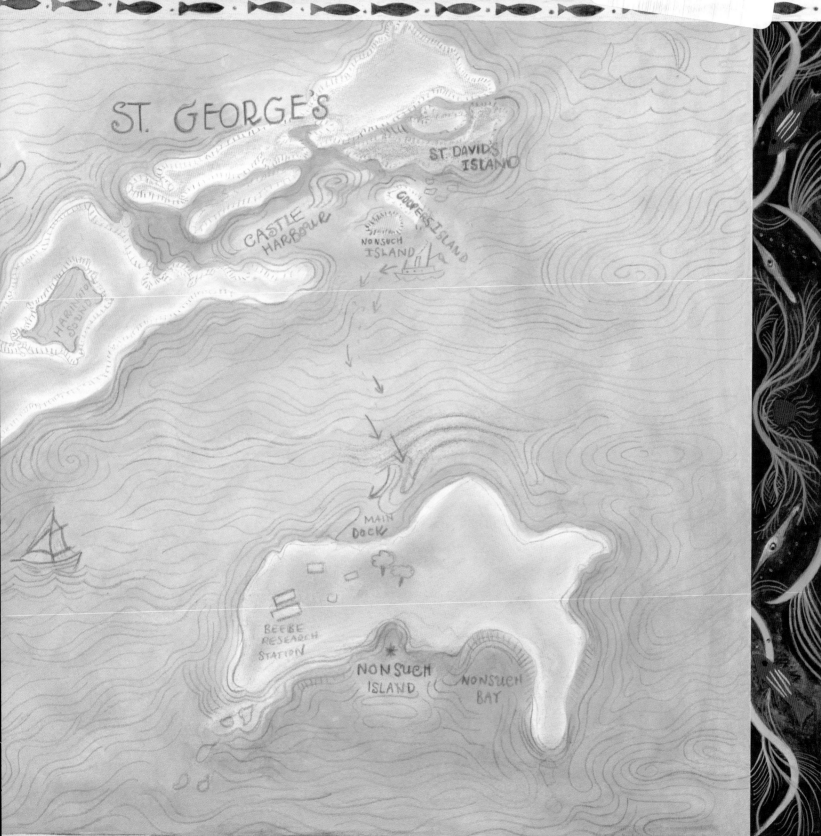

ST. GEORGE'S

ST. DAVID'S
ISLAND

COOPER'S ISLAND

CASTLE
HARBOUR

NONSUCH
ISLAND

HARRINGTON
SOUND

MAIN
DOCK

BEEBE
RESEARCH
STATION

NONSUCH
ISLAND

NONSUCH
BAY

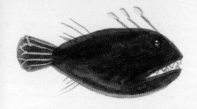
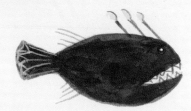

To Will and Scott, my wonderful sons, and our adventures.
To Amy, my editor and friend, who also loves art and oceans.

I would like to thank Edith Widder, PhD, CEO and senior scientist at the
Ocean Research & Conservation Association, Inc.; Madeleine Thompson,
director, Library & Archives, at the Wildlife Conservation Society; Brett
Dion, archivist and digital assets manager at the Wildlife Conservation
Society; Jennifer Harbster, head of the Science Reference Section at the
Library of Congress; Heather C. Thomas, reference librarian in the Serial
and Government Publications Division at the Library of Congress; and
Eve Godet Thomas, director of programming and engagement at the
Bermuda National Gallery. —J.W.H.

For my beloved Grandma Lou. —M.S.

Text copyright © 2024 Jeanne Walker Harvey
Illustrations copyright © 2024 Melodie Stacey

Book design by Melissa Nelson Greenberg
These images were created using gouache, watercolor, pastels, and colored pencils.

Published in 2024 by CAMERON KIDS, an imprint of ABRAMS. All rights reserved. No portion of this book
may be reproduced, stored in a retrieval system, or transmitted in any form or by any means, mechanical,
electronic, photocopying, recording, or otherwise, without written permission from the publisher.

Library of Congress Cataloging-in-Publication Data available.

ISBN: 978-1-949480-28-3

Printed in China

10 9 8 7 6 5 4 3 2 1

CAMERON KIDS books are available at special discounts when purchased in quantity for premiums
and promotions as well as fundraising or educational use. Special editions can also be created to
specifications. For details, contact specialsales@abramsbooks.com or the address below.

ABRAMS
Children's Books

ABRAMS The Art of Books
195 Broadway, New York, NY 10007
abramsbooks.com

ELSE B. IN THE SEA

THE WOMAN WHO PAINTED THE WONDERS OF THE DEEP

BY JEANNE WALKER HARVEY • ILLUSTRATED BY MELODIE STACEY

cameron kids

The first time Else B. climbed down
the long metal ladder dangling off the boat
into the ocean by Bermuda,
her hands trembled.
It was 1930, and few had ventured
deep into the sea before.
Else, who loved to paint the natural world,
had only dreamed of such an adventure.
She felt a frisson of fear.

Faraway from her New York City home,
Else's dream had come true.
She was hired to paint
what a famous scientist, William Beebe,
might see in the deep waters from his bathysphere.
At that time, little was known about life
in the great depths of the ocean.

Painting was Else's passion.
When she was a lonesome girl in Germany,
art comforted her.
She won awards and exhibited her work.

But for almost twenty years,
Else had to put aside her dreams of painting.
First as a bride when she immigrated to America.
Next as a young widow raising her daughter.

To prepare for her new job,
Else wanted to paint the ocean firsthand.
So she set off to work,
descending as far as she could by herself.

The enormous copper helmet
placed on Else's shoulders
made her feel like an outer space explorer.
She sank into the choppy, turquoise water.
Through the glass window,
she spotted in the distance
the sparkling stretch of sand,
leaning cedar trees,
and tiny white buildings
on Nonsuch Island where she worked.

The rippling surface distorted
the familiar world
as she entered
an unknown one.

Once she plunged deeper,
she felt weightless, as if free flying.
When her ears began to throb from the pressure,
Else remembered to swallow hard
to ease the pain.

She quickly forgot her discomfort
when the magnificent valley appeared below.
Peaks of tall coral reefs, swaying sea plumes,
and slender purple sea fans.
Else's feet touched the softest sand imaginable.
She felt she had arrived in a magical fairyland
six fathoms below the surface.
Fantastic castle formations faded
into blue, shadowy silhouettes.
Sunbeams glittered in the warm water.

Peaceful but eerie.

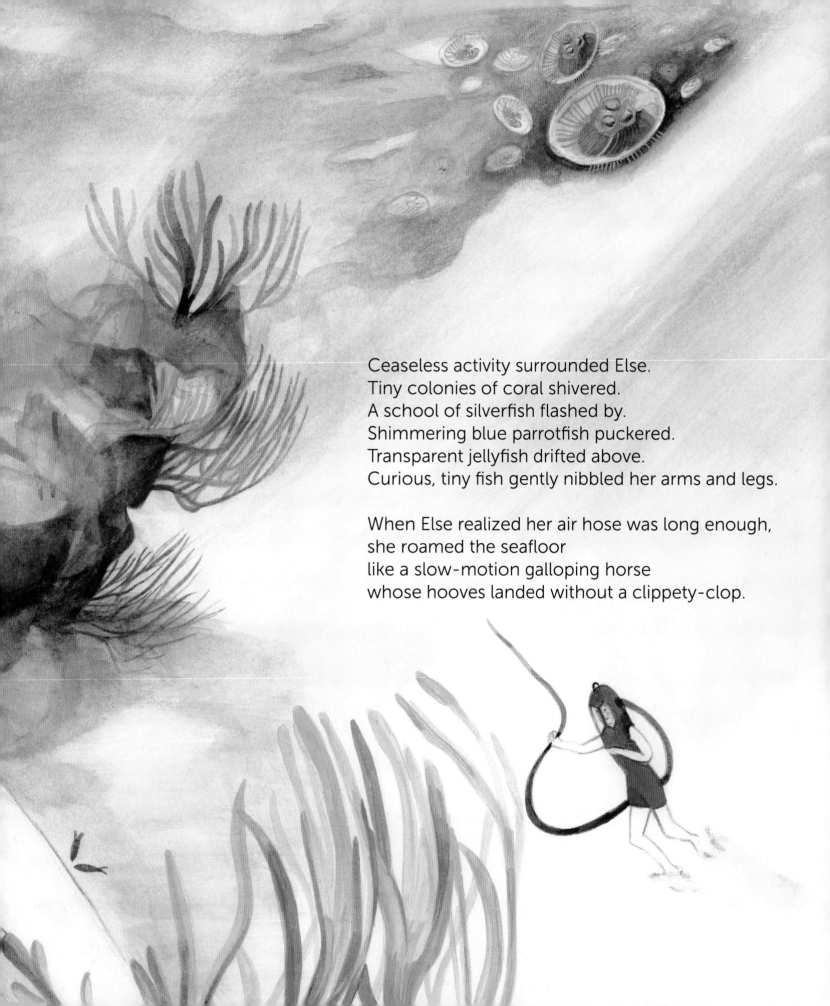

Ceaseless activity surrounded Else.
Tiny colonies of coral shivered.
A school of silverfish flashed by.
Shimmering blue parrotfish puckered.
Transparent jellyfish drifted above.
Curious, tiny fish gently nibbled her arms and legs.

When Else realized her air hose was long enough,
she roamed the seafloor
like a slow-motion galloping horse
whose hooves landed without a clippety-clop.

With a steel pencil on a zinc plate,
Else scratched out pictures of what she saw.
She was careful not to tilt her head,
or her heavy helmet would tumble off,
and she would need to shoot to the surface for air.

As Else glanced around her,
she discovered something.
Certain colors were missing
from a mere two fathoms up.
She could still spot the delicious hues
of green, bright yellow, and orange.
But the purple gorgonian,
the red sea anemone,
and even her favorite red bathing suit
now looked gray.

Determined to show how color
changed in the ocean depths,
Else experimented with ways
to paint underwater.

She found that oil paint didn't mix with saltwater
during her half-hour sea explorations.

At first, she plopped dollops of paint
inside a metal washtub.
But reaching far into the tub proved awkward.
Else developed a better method
by attaching her canvas to an iron music stand,
lowered from the boat on a rope.

Her weighted palette with dabs of paint
and attached brushes
floated within reach.

From what she learned,
Else created a color guide for the scientist.

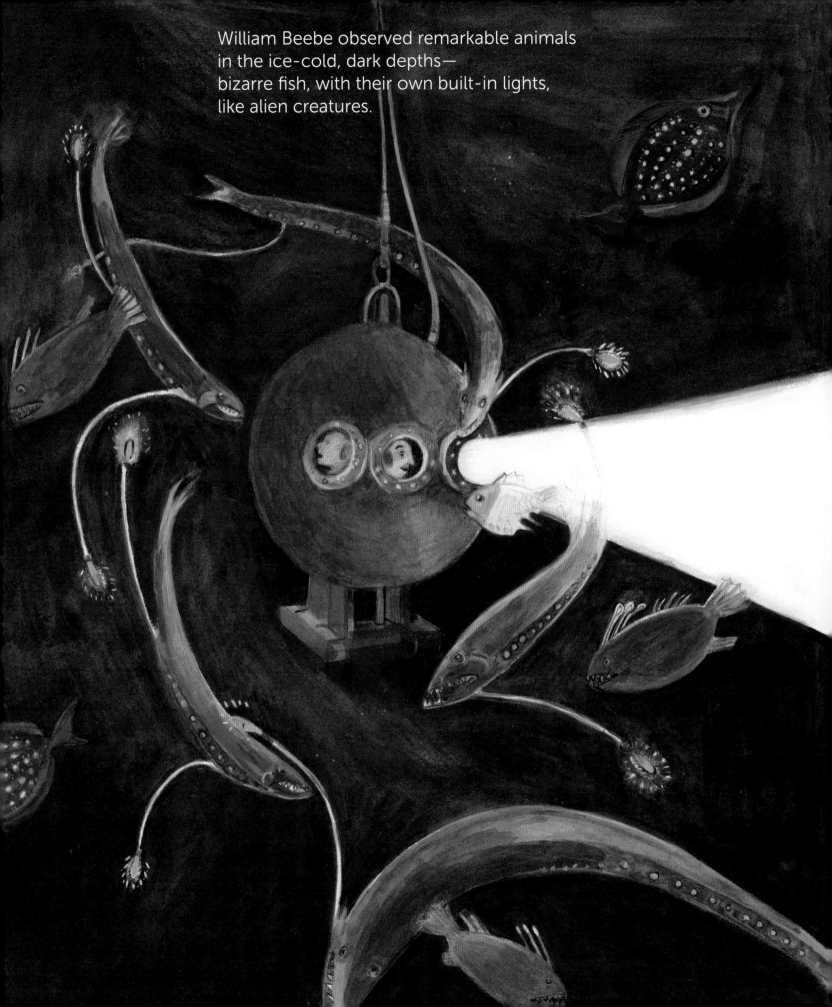

William Beebe observed remarkable animals
in the ice-cold, dark depths—
bizarre fish, with their own built-in lights,
like alien creatures.

Back on land, Else hurried to the shore
whenever the tugboat blew its horn
to announce the arrival of the creatures
trawled from the ocean depths.

Else dashed off quick watercolor sketches
before the shimmer of the fish
and the glow of their luminous organs
disappeared in mere minutes,
like a shower of shooting stars.

Else was saddened, knowing these creatures
would never again be as astonishing
as they were in their deep ocean habitat.
She vowed to honor their lives
by painting them with great care.

With a microscope,
Else studied the structure
of the fish and noted details,
such as fin rays and photophores.

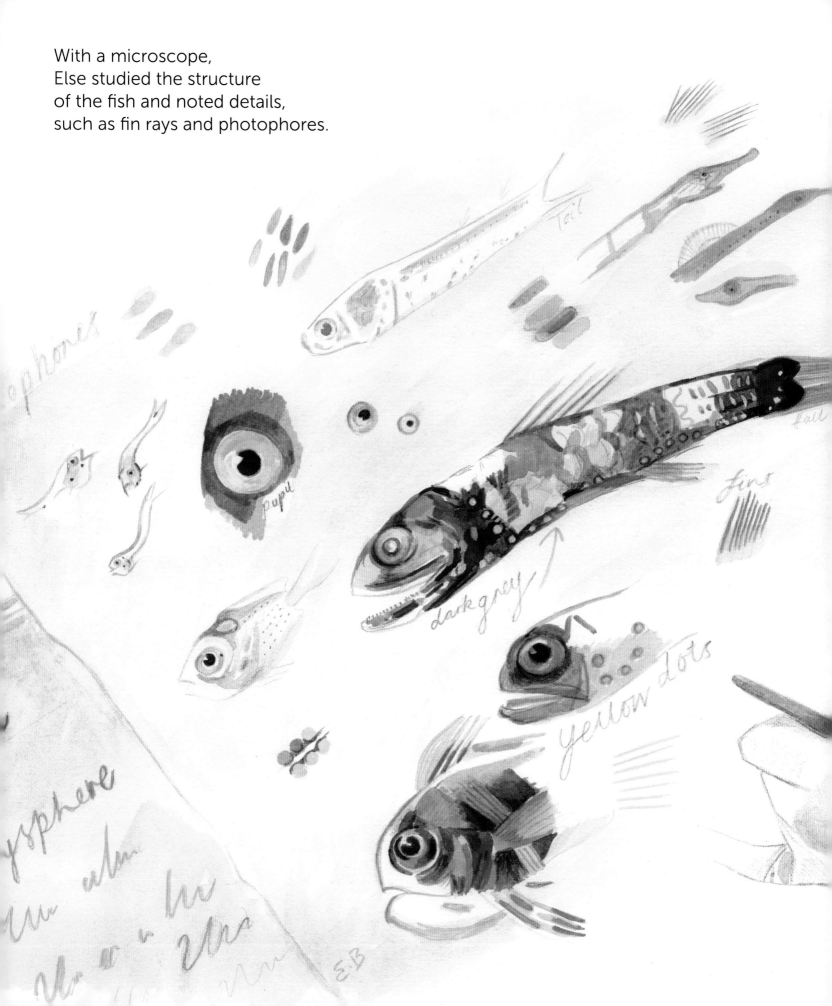

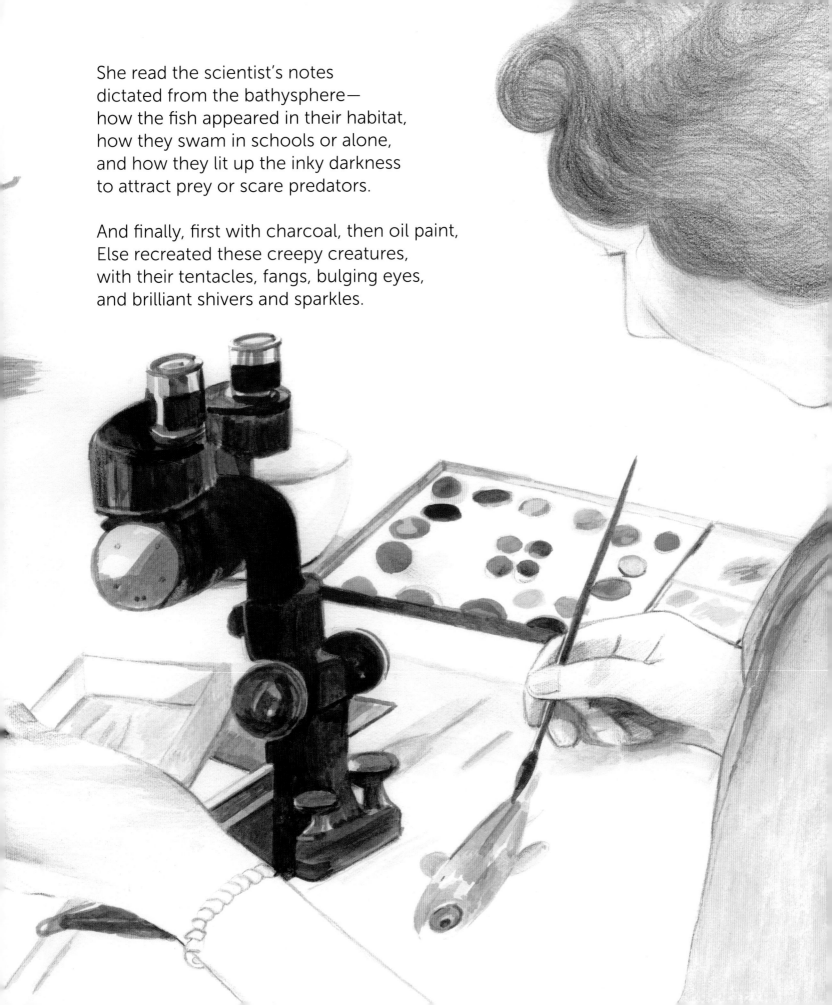

She read the scientist's notes
dictated from the bathysphere—
how the fish appeared in their habitat,
how they swam in schools or alone,
and how they lit up the inky darkness
to attract prey or scare predators.

And finally, first with charcoal, then oil paint,
Else recreated these creepy creatures,
with their tentacles, fangs, bulging eyes,
and brilliant shivers and sparkles.

Gulper Eel
Black Swallower
Three-Starred Anglerfish
Silver Hatchetfish
Pygmy Round-Mouths
Needle Heads
Orange-Lighted Finger-Squid
Swivel-Toothed Dragonfish
Lanternfish
Exploding Scarlet Shrimp
Telescope-Eyed Fish
Shining-Toothed Angler
Black Whalelet
Scarlet Arrow Worms
Five-Lined Constellation Fish

Exploding Scarlet Shrimp

Great Gulper Eel

Lantern Fish

Saber-toothed Viper fish

Shining-toothed Angler

Scarlet Arrow Worms

Needle Heads

Telescope-Eyed fish

Five-lined constellation fish

silver Hatchet fish

Pygmy Round-mouths

Three-starred angler fish

Black Whalelet

Black Swallower

Orange-Lighted Finger-squid

Swivel-toothed Dragonfish

EB

When summer ended,
the bathysphere diving season ceased.
Else left Nonsuch Island
and ascended the ramp of a steamship
heading back to New York City.
She proudly carried her passel of paintings
to deliver to a popular magazine
that planned to publish them,
along with the words of the scientist.

Else felt an unfathomable joy.
Her paintings would give people
a way to escape their worries
during a hard time back in America.
A way to travel, in their imaginations,
on a marvelous underwater journey,
as impossible and exciting
as soaring to the sparkling stars above.

All because Else B. dared
to take those first steps
down the ladder
and into the deep dark sea.

AUTHOR'S NOTE

Else Bostelmann's story is one of art illuminating the science and beauty of the ocean. I was inspired to write this book when I read an article by oceanographer Edith Widder about Else's 1930s paintings of deep-sea bioluminescent creatures discovered off the coast of Bermuda. Else's striking paintings reminded me of my own Bermuda underwater adventure in a submarine, where I witnessed stunning marine life and sea vistas. And her paintings also reminded me of the glorious blue shimmer of glowing microorganisms I've seen in the wake of my friend's sailboat in the Puget Sound in Washington.

Else was a classically trained artist born in Germany in 1882. When she was nearing fifty years old, Else was hired to paint the amazing deep-sea creatures that the scientist William Beebe encountered on his momentous bathysphere expeditions off the coast of Bermuda (1930–1934), including a record half-mile descent.

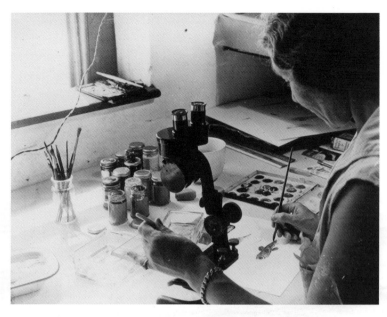

Else Bostelmann painting at Bermuda expedition laboratory. © Wildlife Conservation Society. Reproduced by permission of the WCS Archives.

At a time before television or high-resolution underwater photography was invented, Else was the one who brought Beebe's famous descriptions of his discoveries to light with her amazing paintings. Her paintings, published in the popular *National Geographic* magazine in 1931 and 1934 during the Great Depression, allowed millions of people the opportunity to visually experience and appreciate a new world with previously unimaginable bioluminescent creatures.

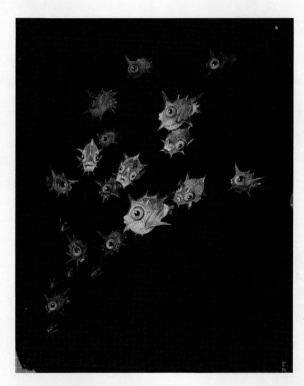

Else's painting of young ocean sunfish. © Wildlife Conservation Society. Reproduced by permission of the WCS Archives.

During that era, Beebe's discoveries were sometimes discredited because he hired a number of female scientists for his New York Zoological Society (now the Wildlife Conservation Society) expeditions. However, over the years, Beebe's discoveries of numerous deep-sea creatures and the details of many of Else's paintings have been proven accurate. Several of the women on these expeditions became leaders in the oceanographic field.

The names of the deep-sea fish used in this book reflect the labels of Else's paintings as they appeared in the 1931 and 1934 *National Geographic* editions. Over the past ninety years, some of these names have been retained or modified, including the Latin references, as more discoveries have been made.

After the deep-sea expedition with Beebe, during which she painted hundreds of fish images, Else provided more illustrations for *National Geographic* magazine and illustrated fourteen children's nature books. She died in 1961.

I believe Else's experiences show how one person can make a difference, and every person's contribution is important behind the scenes of major discoveries. And as Else said, "No modern adventure can surpass the supreme joy of exploring [the deep sea's] unique grandeur."

I HOPE ELSE'S STORY INSPIRES US TO CARE FOR AND PROTECT OUR MARVELOUS OCEANS AND CREATURES, SO MUCH OF WHICH IS STILL UNKNOWN.

UNDERWATER COLOR SPECTRUM

The white light we see is actually composed of a spectrum of colors: violet, indigo, blue, green, yellow, orange, and red, all with varying wavelengths. However, there is a rapid loss of light intensity underwater. As Else observed, red (with the longest wavelength) appears to fade to grey the fastest.

A FATHOM is a nautical unit of measurement

originally connected to Dutch and German words that mean "something which embraces" and "outstretched arms." The span of a man's outstretched arms is about six feet, which is why one fathom equals six feet.

MATH CONVERSION TABLE

1 fathom = 6 feet = 1.8288 meters
2 fathoms = 12 feet = 3.6576 meters
4 fathoms = 24 feet = 7.3152 meters
6 fathoms = 36 feet = 10.9728 meters

BIOLUMINESCENCE

I'm entranced by the way Else chose to paint the deep-sea creatures on black backgrounds to highlight their amazing glow-in-the-dark characteristics, such as a festive string of lights along the side of a fish or a tantalizing glowing tentacle.

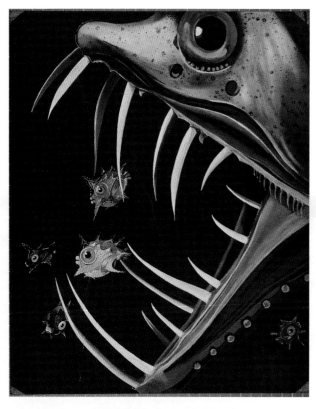

Else's painting of saber-toothed viperfish pursuing young ocean sunfish.
© Wildlife Conservation Society. Reproduced by permission of the WCS Archives.

Creatures living in the great depths of the ocean produce light to hunt, confuse predators, and communicate. This amazing phenomenon, called bioluminescence, occurs through a chemical reaction that happens when luciferin, a light-emitting compound, reacts with luciferase, a kind of enzyme, in an organism's body. Bioluminescence mostly appears as blue-green, probably because the short wavelengths of blue and green light travel longer distances in the sea and were therefore favored by natural selection. A few animals emit red light, which they can see but other deep-sea dwellers cannot, allowing them to use their bioluminescence to hunt.

Scientists have used what they've learned about ocean bioluminescence to help study diseases. For example, green fluorescent protein, first obtained from a jellyfish, is used to light up and track diseased cells, such as cancer, in humans.

An estimated 76 percent of all ocean animals luminesce, and in fish alone, there are about 1,500 known bioluminescent species. Who knows how many others are waiting to be discovered in the deep dark sea?

SELECTED SOURCES

Bostelmann, Else. "Luminous Life in the Depths of the Sea." *National Geographic*, June 1931.
——. "Flashes from Ocean Deeps—A Lightless World," *National Geographic*, December 1934.
——. "With an Artist at the Bottom of the Sea." *The Christian Science Monitor*, July 1935.
——. "Notes from an Undersea Studio Off Bermuda." *Country Life*, February 1939.
Dion, Mark, Katherine McLeod, and Madeleine Thompson. *Exploratory Works: Drawings from the Department of Tropical Research Field Expeditions.* New York: The Drawing Center, 2017. Exhibition catalog.
Widder, Edith. 2016. "The Fine Art of Exploration." *Oceanography* 29 (4): 170–177. https://doi.org/10.5670/oceanog.2016.86.